Contents

A Speedy Flier

A dragonfly flaps its strong wings.

The **insect** has big eyes and a long body.

How did it get this way?

A DRAGONFLY GROWS

by Rex Ruby

Consultant: Beth Gambro,
Reading Specialist, Yorkville, Illinois

BEARPORT
PUBLISHING

Minneapolis, Minnesota

Teaching Tips

Before Reading

- Look at the cover of the book. Discuss the picture and the title.

- Ask readers to brainstorm a list of what they already know about dragonflies. What can they expect to see in the book?

- Go on a picture walk, looking through the pictures to discuss vocabulary and make predictions about the text.

During Reading

- Read for purpose. Encourage readers to think about how a dragonfly grows as they are reading.

- Ask readers to look for the details of the book. What are they learning about different stages of the growing process?

- If readers encounter an unknown word, ask them to look at the sounds in the word. Then, ask them to look at the rest of the page. Are there any clues to help them understand?

After Reading

- Encourage readers to pick a buddy and reread the book together.

- Ask readers to name two things that happen as a dragonfly grows. Find the pages that tell about these things.

- Ask readers to write or draw something they learned about dragonflies.

Credits

Cover and title page, © Teresa Bass/Shutterstock; 3, © Hanoi/Adobe Stock; 5, © Olesia Novitckaia/Adobe Stock; 7, © Robert Schneider/Adobe Stock; 8–9, © Martin/Adobe Stock; 11, © Young Swee Ming/Shutterstock; 13, © Robert Thompson/Minden Pictures; 15, © Stephen Dalton/Minden Pictures; 16–17, © blickwinkel/Alamy Stock Photo; 19L, © David E Lester/Alamy Stock Photo; 19R, © David E Lester/Alamy Stock Photo; 21, © Biscut/iStock; 22TR, © Benny Trapp/Adobe Stock; 22ML, © yod67/Adobe Stock and © Jackson Photography/Adobe Stock and © Paulrommer/Adobe Stock and © Chase D'Animulls/Adobe Stock and © Butterfly Hunter/Shutterstock and © xpixel/Shutterstock; 22BR, © Ivan Synieokov/Adobe Stock; 23TL, © Nina Basharova/Adobe Stock; 23TM, © Aekkaphum/Adobe Stock; 23TR, © Anton Kozyrev/Adobe Stock; 23BL, © E. Boros/Adobe Stock; 23BM, © Tonia Graves/ Alamy Stock Photo; 23BR, © VitalisG/iStock

See BearportPublishing.com for our statement on Generative AI Usage.

Library of Congress Cataloging-in-Publication Data is available at www.loc.gov or upon request from the publisher.

ISBN: 979-8-89232-995-8 (hardcover)
ISBN: 979-8-89577-426-7 (paperback)
ISBN: 979-8-89577-112-9 (ebook)

For more information, write to Bearport Publishing, 3500 American Blvd W, Suite 150, Bloomington, MN 55431.

5

Dragonflies start out as tiny eggs.

These eggs form after two dragonflies **mate**.

A mother dragonfly lays many eggs at once.

She may drop them in the water.

Sometimes, she lays them on water plants.

A dragonfly laying eggs

9

Each egg has an **embryo** growing inside.

That embryo will become a dragonfly one day.

Eggs

11

After a few days, the eggs **hatch**.

The baby dragonflies are called **nymphs**.

These little bugs live in the water.

Say nymphs like NIMFZ

A dragonfly nymph eats a lot.

It feeds on other insects in the water.

Sometimes it eats small fish, too.

The dragonfly gets bigger.

It sheds its skin as it grows.

This is called **molting**.

A nymph molts many times.

Old skin

A nymph

17

Then, the nymph leaves the water.

It molts one last time.

A dragonfly with wings crawls out!

At first, the wings are wet.

They become dry after a few hours.

Then, the dragonfly takes off!

Dragonfly Facts

Dragonflies are the fastest flying insects on Earth.

There are thousands of kinds of dragonflies.

Dragonflies can fly in place in the air like helicopters!

22

Glossary

embryo an animal in the first stage of growth

hatch to break out of an egg

insect a small animal that has six legs and three main body parts

mate to come together to have young

molting shedding an old skin so a new one can form

nymphs young dragonflies that live in water

Index

Read More

Rose, Rachel. *Dragonfly Migration (Weather Makes Them Move).* Minneapolis: Bearport Publishing Company, 2024.

Thompson, Kim. *Dragonflies (Bugs in My Yard).* Coral Springs, FL: Seahorse Publishing, 2022.

Learn More Online

1. Go to **FactSurfer.com** or scan the QR code below.
2. Enter "**Dragonflies Grow**" into the search box.
3. Click on the cover of this book to see a list of websites.

About the Author

Rex Ruby lives in Minnesota with his family. He likes looking for dragonflies at the pond near his house.